What a shit book!

I'll become a

youtuber

Chiquitita_63

Chiquitita tell me the truth.

Torremolinos 63

So, let's begin. I suppose I should write kind of an introduction or something like that, but not before giving thousands of "thank you" to all those people who helped me to build this great piece of shit, I mean this book, the one that you with no guns on your head, decided to buy (I hope it wasn't your money), despite my warnings.

After this stupid presentation, it's time now to explain the intentions of this book. (Let's call this a "book", not for the new knowledge you'll find in it, but for being made of paper and having pages with numbers at the bottom.

Anyway, the intentions are waiting for you in the following lines, because I don't want to lie to you. This is the biggest mountain made of shit you will find in a very long time.

Intentions:

One,

    write a book.

Two,

    sell my book.

Three,

    warn you before number two about not buy-
ing my book.

Four,

    doing something creative before waking up.

Five,

    No, there aren't five. Just four.

Ok, six,

   make you to understand that life deserves to be lived out of internet, screens or any piece shit created by some bored people who want to write a book before waking up.

There's nothing here.

Sorry, nothing here.

HERE NEITHER

Calm. We have to start step by step.

Don't get nervous.

No rush.

Don't flee.

In this page there's a giant dot.

You see? It's starting to become interesting.

dot

This book is made by a youtuber, so I guess you should break this page and throw it away while laughing like a witch.

I haven't written anything here. I supposed you were going to break the page and throw it away. While laughing like a witch.

PAGE UNDER CONSTRUCTION,

KEEP GOING.

DON'T STOP.

Get a snot. Put it in middle of the circle,

name it and write the name below.

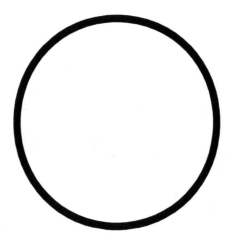

Hi, I'm a snot. My name is.................

There's nothing in this page.

What for?

When you close the book, there

will be a snot here soon.

Just reminding you bought this book (I hope it wasn't with your own money)

You have contributed to the deforestation of the World. One less tree thanks to you. Sleep well.

Write your boss' name. Go to bathroom enjoy and defecate. Then, use this page to clean your bottom. How do you feel having your boss name on your ass plenty of shit? What a sensation! Your welcome for the idea.

I DON'T HATE THONGS,
BUT I HATE WHEN MY
TIGHT PANTIES GET IN MY
ASS, LIKE A THONG.

Why do I call myself Chiquitita_63?

Ten minutes ago I was listening to a famous song. Do you know ABBA? There's a song "Chiquitita tell me what's wrong...". So, I chose "chiquitita". Why "63". There's a mvie called Torremolinos 63 (I think that's the name.) I think I watched it once, I'm not sure. Anyway, I remembered the movie and added the number 63. Chiquitita_63.

Cool, right?

I saw a monkey once. We were at the zoo. I didn't belong to there. Just visiting. He was putting a finger in the ass.

I don't know, he looked bored. However, about putting a finger in the ass. Maybe it wasn't so boring. Maybe I'll try next time I'm bored.

«Hope of the Pain is the aim of our soul.»

I've just invented this sentence. I wanted to create a philosophic phrase plenty of metaphysical knowledge.

Most of the times I don't know what do thore sentences mean when I read them. However, I don't know why butI feel lucky of reading them.

Do you want a silly joke? I don't care your answer. Here's the joke.

Why do dragons sleep during the day?

So they can fight knights.

Not laughing? Come on! It's good!

I don't ever use these symbols to write.

I wanted to give them a chance.

$ & * [ ] } > <

This is your page, dudes. I haven't forgotten you. Maybe there should be an international day for the forgotten symbols. I kow it would be useless, but everyday is the international day of something. Why not, symbols.

Here you have two little ducks.

Are you asking me why?

Why not? Do you have anything against ducks?

Ok, that's what I thought.

What and when was your last selfie?

Mine it's me (of course) behind a plant.

I wasn't inspired that day.

And yours?

I don't care, don't tell me, don't even write it.

I won't read it.

Hey! This is the page number 24. I'm becoming an excellent writer (I'm joking.) But I still can do it better. Keep reading. I can prove it.

This page contains a super very important message written with a special invisible ink. Just intelligent people can read it.

Wow, what a message!!

What! You couldn't read it! I'm sorry. I didn't want to embarrass you.

Just keep studying. Maybe one day you'll be ready for the message.

Or maybe not..?

Go to page 63 directly from here and check it out.

You'll see something really curious.

Are you angry for the joke before? You have to admit it's been funny.

Ok, something to learn.

Don't say I didn't teach you anything.

No one can lick his own elbow.

Oh my God! You did it? Really!?

You tried to lick you elbow!?

I knew you would ask me more.

Ok, listen.

People fart everyday. That's a fact. But how many times?

An average of 14 times per day.

I love farting when I'm alone.

I love strong farts.

I like smelly farts when I'm not alone (I know, I'm evil.)

What a lucky animals!

Frogs spend the entire day belching and no one tell them off.

When was last time you belched? Have a soda and practice.

Try to say the alphabet while belching.

I'm trying to write every page with a different characters. I'm fed up of the tyranny of Times News Roman and her friend Arial.

This page is ready you to write your best ideas to become rich.

_____

_____

_____

_____

_____

_____

_____

_____

_____

_____

_____

_____

_____

_____

_____

_____

_____

_____

You haven't written anything, right?

The page before, I mean.

I don't know why but I knew it.

Keep reading this sort of book is much better than planning a better future for yourself.

Fucking lazy

It's too hot outside. I have to wake up and close the window.

Here I am again. The window is closed.

Get into a room full of people. (If you are already inside, don't get in, because you are already inside). Stand up among them, rise your hands and arms like if you were a ghost or a drunk dancer and shout like a ghost: "This is a dreeeaaam."

I would pay to see their faces.

My mom is calling me. Breakfast is ready since ten minutes ago.

Breakfast is in my stomach.

Let's continue.

Kerfuffle

Ragamuffin

Gobbledygook

What a curious words, aren't they?

Do you know what they mean?

I don't.

Do you know what can you do? You can take this book, go out and throw it up. At the same time you must shout very loudly so that everyone can hear you: "Fly, little bird! Fly, flyyy!!"

Ufff! It's really hard to be a youtuber or influencer and writing a book. I'm exhausted.

Another joke? No?

Ok, here it comes.

I dreamed I was forced to eat a giant marshmallow. When I woke up, my pillow was gone.

Have you ever realized the worst jokes are the best ones? I mean. It's impossible to remember a good joke. You just remember it was good and that you laughed a lot. However, it's really easy to remember the bad ones. Every time someone ask you to tell a joke, you just can remember the bad ones. The reason is that the brain is very intelligent. They are the perfect bullet to use every time someone ask you for a joke. And don't worry. They are so bad that people will laugh. Meanwhile they'll tell you the joke was so bad that was actually good.

Draw a picture

Enjoy the white colour of this page.

How to become a youtuber.

You were thinking I wouldn't give you any advices to become a youtuber? Here they are.

- First,

you need a gadget with camera and access to internet. It doesn't need to be yours.
- Second,

create a youtube or instagram account.
- Third,

record a video. Say whatever you want.
- Fourth,

upload the video.
- Fifth,

remind your folloers to subscribe to your channel.
- Sixth,

write a book.

- Seventh,

no. That's all. Just six.

Have you realized you have already

read 52 pages?

I was bored when I wrote this book,

but you win me.

Throw this book away.

Maybe you should have done it long time ago.

Have you ever tried farting and belching at the same time?

Try it. If someone watches you, blame me. Say that the book told you to do it. Say this book has all the answers.

Nothing here.

Just the sentence "nothing here" and a dot.

In
the
next
page
I'm
going
to
write
an
"M".

I have to work tomorrow. What a shit!

At least, today is not tomorrow. Good!

You see? Always look on the bright side of life.

You liked the idea of writing the letter "M" several

pages before, right?

Next page is for you. DO the same.

Make a hole in this page.

If you do it well,

another hole will appear in the next page.

:-)

What did I tell you?

What a hole!

.

Oh my God! I can't believe it!
You did it! You came here from
page 27!!!

If I say that I want you to jump
from a bridge down, will you do it?

In this page and the next one write a letter to your bed (yes, to your bed. You spend so many nights together... it deserves a love letter)

_____

_____

_____

_____

_____

_____

_____

_____

_____

_____

_____

_____

_____

_____

_____

So, that's all folks!

The book is finished.

No, really. That's all. There's nothing else. You can close if you want, or maybe you can start again.

What? You didn't like the book? I told you. I warned you. But you didn't trust my words, the title and maybe the comments of all of those brains who dared to buy the book before you.

I know it won't be easy to find a new purpose in your life, but this is what it is. Don't worry. I do trust you. I know you'll find the way to keep going ahead.

What about me? I'm becoming a youtuber. So we'll see each other soon, very very soon...